MW00939986

MY ESCAPE FROM A PADDED CELL

An Inspirational Memoir by a Person with a Traumatic Brain Injury

Michael Alan Northrop

TABLE OF CONTENTS

PART TWO – My Lessons in Life

SPECIAL THANKS

I owe special thanks to two individuals who helped me edit this book. Yvona Fast is an author/editor and friend who read each part of this book and gave me several suggestions to improve my writing and clarity. She has written and had published two books: *Employment for Individuals with Asperger's Syndrome or Non-Verbal Learning Disability: Stories and Strategies,* and *Garden Gourmet*, a cookbook spotlighting locally-grown ingredients. She also edited her mother's book, *My Nine Lives*, about her experiences during the Holocaust.

I also received intensive organizational assistance from a professional as I finalized this book. His name is Michael Cochran, Ph.D., and he does Independent Living Skills Training with me through the Traumatic Brain Injury Medicaid Waiver. With his assistance, I became more independent editing my writing.

I also need to thank some very special people in my life. Mom, I love you! You helped me develop my can-do attitude. I cannot forget my amazing wife, Cheryl. You are my miracle from the Lord. I have been receiving services from Sunmount DDSO, The Adirondack Arc, the NENYCSP/TBI Center in Plattsburgh and North Country Home Services. I will never be able to thank any of you enough.

DEDICATIONS

This book is dedicated to two of the most powerful people in my life–my Lord and Savior, Jesus Christ, and my mother, Suzanne McGibeny. My mother is with the Lord now because on February 18, 2008, she lost an almost quarter century battle with heart and lung disease. I acquired my resilience from her.

My relationship with the Lord has grown stronger ever since February 1997. I considered suicide after receiving my second rejection for Federal disability benefits. I remember my mother brought me to the emergency room and I was eventually brought to a crisis residence. The Lord used a janitor that evening to transform my life. After we talked about my problems, he said, "Sometimes, you just gotta believe." His words made me realize I had to put God in control.

For these reasons and because I love them so much, this book is dedicated to the Lord Jesus Christ and my mother, Suzanne McGibeny. They have helped me in countless ways.

ABOUT THE AUTHOR

This book outlines numerous obstacles I have overcome in my life. After developing very severe asthma as a baby, a brain injury at age ten severely damaged my memory. It was very difficult, but I earned a Bachelor's Degree in Psychology from Utica College of Syracuse University in 1996. Several stresses culminated in a near suicide attempt in 1997, but then something miraculous happened. The Lord entered my life!

Three months later, I had successfully moved out into my original hometown, a small hamlet in

Upstate New York. After qualifying to receive assistance living with my disability, I chose to move to a larger town. On July 4, 2004, I suffered a massive cerebral aneurysm and stroke, which made living very difficult but also strengthened my resolve. I started working at a local supermarket, and eventually got hooked up in a job organizing support groups for individuals with developmental disabilities. I met my miracle from the Lord through that job, and on October 3, 2009, I married her! Unfortunately, my brain injury eventually proved itself too involved to allow me to continue that job.

After that, I stopped looking for work and eventually qualified for intensive services by switching to a different treatment system. I started receiving supports designed to help me adapt to my brain injury, and eventually started using one of those supports to help guide the writing of this book. During that time, I attended a day treatment program for individuals with traumatic brain injuries for a couple of years. Then I started looking for work again and eventually found a good job doing janitorial work for the Olympic Regional Development Authority in Lake Placid. All the while, I kept gradually revising this book. Finally, in October 2016, Cheryl and I chose to move to Lake Placid and have enjoyed it tremendously.

I hope that my story inspires you to not let obstacles slow you down on your path to success.

DISCLAIMER

This book was originally written in 2005 and published in 2006. I revised it to improve its quality and to include everything that has happened to me since then. My brain injury was evident in my original version because chapters four and six had the same text!

With Yvona and Mike's help, I became aware of numerous instances in my original manuscript where my brain injury affected my writing. Mike showed me how my disability impairs how clearly my thinking gets translated into words. Mike and Yvona helped me discover several redundancies, instances where my thoughts strayed off-topic and places I got too wordy. I realized I didn't always communicate as clearly as possible. I have done substantial editing, but if you catch any errors in my writing, please realize they are a direct result of my brain injury. In fact, I think they might tell you as much about my injury as my words do!

MY PERSPECTIVE ON LIFE

I have moved past several challenging circumstances in my life. They all made me the person I am today. You will read about how a brain injury damaged my memory, how my vision became compromised, how I overcame struggles in college, how I got out of a sheltered workshop, and how I survived a cerebral aneurysm and stroke. You will also read about the unique way I met my wife, how I switched my system of supports and how I got my current job.

All my experiences share one thing in common: I saw things as challenges instead of obstacles. I never stopped challenging my abilities and neither should you. "But what if I fail?" you might ask. My answer is simple: "How will you ever know what you can do until you try?" Let's face it. None of us have succeeded at everything we have done. Trial and error will give you a realistic perspective of what you can and can't do.

In 1996, I graduated from Utica College of Syracuse University. Starting out, I knew I had a poor memory but I was excited about proving to myself what I could accomplish. When it became difficult, doubt tried to creep in but I didn't let it. I tried even harder! Being truly honest, I received a few accommodations to make it a little easier, but so what? We all need a little help occasionally.

Here are two specific examples of how I saw circumstances in my life not as limitations but challenges. During the aneurysm surgery, I had a stroke that weakened my right arm and hand. Holding onto a fork or a pen was almost impossible at first, but I didn't give up. After living with my family during the summer, I chose to accept a recommendation by my support team to live in supported housing briefly to adjust to independence, then used my supports to transition back into my apartment. I used those challenges to energize my drive to keep going and was successful.

My life perspective has also been formed by the jobs I have held in the past. After moving out on my own, my first real competitive job was bagging groceries at a local grocery store.

During my five years there, I proved I can work competitively. I then moved on to a job leading groups of people with disabilities. This was exciting at first but soon became overwhelming because there was too much to organize and travel was difficult. I currently work on a janitorial crew for the Olympic Regional Development Authority in Lake Placid. It is a good job for me because it is very routine and I have co-workers and supervisors who have looked past my disabilities to see my potential instead.

My perspective on life is also based on my salvation through my Lord, Jesus Christ. I have gotten through everything in life knowing He is there for me whenever I need Him. I have read *The Holy Bible* a few times and use its wisdom to shape my life. I know nothing will ever happen to me that I cannot handle with His help. I realize that many people do not have faith beliefs like mine, but please use whatever belief you do have to help you in the times when you need it.

I chose to entitle this book *My Escape from a Padded Cell* for several reasons. As a child, I saw myself as less capable than my peers because asthma restricted my activity a lot. After a seizure at age ten permanently damaged my memory, I became dependent on people. I recovered from an aneurysm and stroke at age thirty. I am now confident that my Lord wouldn't have let any of it happen without giving me what I needed to succeed. All of this has given me a positive perspective on life and throughout this whole book I hope you will learn more about it.

PART ONE –

My Life History

CHAPTER 1 –
I Was a Very Sick Kid

I didn't have what you would call a normal childhood. At thirteen months old, I was diagnosed with chronic asthma, which seriously impaired my breathing and forced my mom to take on the role of caregiver. It was almost fate that she had been professionally trained to take care of seriously ill infants. I believe God prepared her for what she would need to do for me.

We lived in Indian Lake, a very small town in northern New York. Because my asthma attacks were so severe and the nearest hospital was an hour away, she knew she could never wait too long to call the ambulance. Because I had to go there so frequently, the nurses became secondary moms to me and saw me through all the developmental stages of childhood. One even taught me how to tie my shoes!

During one of my visits, a nurse did me a special favor. I had a stuffed dog named Henry and carried him around everywhere I went. During one of my hospital visits, one of Henry's legs fell off. I couldn't stop crying! She took me into one of the back rooms where we washed up and put on surgical gloves, gowns, caps and masks. She sewed little Henry's leg back on for me! I picked him right up, hugged him tightly and shouted, "He's new again!"

I learned early in life to accept help from medical professionals instead of fighting them. The nurses and doctors were trying to help me, and although their shots and pills were never fun, they made me feel better. I used to need breathing treatments and quickly realized they also helped me feel a lot better. And as much as I hated having to get needle after needle for bloodwork, injections and IV's, those also helped.

Then at age three, something scary happened. One day, I asked my mother, "What's that funny smell?" She asked me what I meant. I didn't know. I don't remember what happened next but afterwards, I was told I had a grand mal seizure. I was lucky because I didn't lose any abilities from it, but I did have to start a medication I would have to take for the rest of my life.

My health as a child forced me to accept many limitations. I could never ride a bike for more than a few minutes. I always felt left out because I could never play tag, kickball, or active games with friends. When it was too cold or too hot and humid, it was hard to breathe. Mom always had to know when she could let a cold go away on its own, when I needed to see the doctor or when she needed to call the ambulance. These experiences taught me to accept my limitations and move on. Asthma was my only disability until something traumatic happened a little later in childhood.

CHAPTER 2 -
My Biggest Gift from God

My biggest gift from God happened at age ten. Another more severe seizure permanently damaged my memory. I consider this my biggest gift from God because later in life it gave me genuine empathy for others with disabilities. It is very difficult living with my brain injury, but it proves the Lord knew I could handle it. Otherwise, He would never have allowed it to happen.

I have a very strong belief God never gives people any more than He knows they can handle. He trusts our ability to make the most of what we have and is always ready to provide us with His help. All we have to do is ask. I view my disabilities as gifts from God. It is my responsibility to use them to benefit others.

Here's the whole story of how God gave me the gift of a memory disability. It happened during the fall of 1984. I had just started sixth grade in a new school. I tried to blend in as best I could but God had other plans. One morning, I smelled something funny. It was just like the seizure I experienced earlier in life. It was like someone was holding rubbing alcohol right underneath my nose. I have no memory of what happened next because I blacked out. When I woke up, I was in the University of Massachusetts General Hospital. I was told I'd had another seizure.

This seizure affected me much more significantly than the other one. People would tell me something and a few moments later, I did not remember anything about what they had said. I was very scared! I never realized how bad it was until I went back to school. I never had to study much before this seizure, but afterwards I had to spend a lot more time studying because I could not remember things well. I would have to constantly repeat things to myself to remember them.

I also realized I was disoriented everywhere I went. One time, I walked up a set of stairs at the opposite end of my school, thinking they led to the classrooms, only to find janitorial offices. I knew life would be extremely hard from that point onward, but I was not about to give up.

God took away my short-term memory but He left me with precious gifts. I never would have developed the appreciation for people with disabilities and those who support them if I didn't have my disability. It motivates me to help other folks with special needs. Soon after I started living on my own, I started playing music for folks with developmental disabilities three times per week. On Wednesday evenings, I played at their large residence. On Thursdays, I accompanied a sing-a-long at their local day treatment program. And on Fridays, I spent the day at another day program in a nearby town. I played my keyboard for their morning church service, set up place settings and adaptive equipment for three meal groups and entertained in the afternoon on my keyboard. To set up place settings, I created a detailed map for each group, letting me know where each person sat and what type of plate, plate guard, spoon, and cup he or she used. I needed these maps every time because I could never remember any of the details otherwise. After I moved to Saranac Lake, I used my musical gift in other situations. I entertained in five residences for people with disabilities, at the local Adult Center and in my housing complex.

I expanded these volunteering opportunities in January of 2000 when I joined the Board of Directors of the Adirondack Arc, a non-profit agency supporting people with developmental disabilities in northern New York. I joined their human rights committee two years later. I was elected to the Board of Directors of the Self-Advocacy Association of New York State the same year. I also joined the board of directors of another local non-profit disability agency called the Tri-Lakes Center for Independent Living in 2012. In 2014, I joined a local self-advocacy group called The Adirondack Advocators. I want other people with disabilities to succeed like I have, and am proud to be part of making this happen.

My brain injury made it extremely difficult to write this book. After the original version was in print in 2006, I realized I had made a huge error. Chapters four and six had different titles but the same text! I found numerous redundancies where an idea was repeated, often within the same chapter. I had to review everything I wrote to catch instances where I discussed the same thing twice. I had to analyze each sentence to organize my thoughts better, take out any words I didn't need and simplify my vocabulary. Working around these issues to make this book better was one of my biggest accomplishments in my life.

CHAPTER 3 –
The High School Blues

The period between seventh and twelfth grades was the most difficult time in my life because my disabilities affected me so much. Most teenagers love going to malls, but I couldn't because I would get lost. When my classmates got old enough, they all looked forward to getting their driver's licenses. I never could because my orientation was very poor. I envied how my friends were becoming independent, and I hated having to rely on my parents to get me around.

Because my asthma was very bad, I had to get excused from gym each year. My elementary school had been one level, so I never had to navigate stairs. My high school was on three levels and I had only two minutes to get between classes. This often involved going up two flights of stairs and traveling across the school. I always felt rushed going from one class to another, which made my breathing even more difficult. I chose to minimize walking time by carrying several periods' materials, rather than walking to my locker in between each period to exchange them. Just like in elementary school, I often had to miss days because of my asthma, but now my memory issues made it hard to make up work.

Before my seizure in sixth grade, I easily learned the names and faces of my classmates; afterwards, putting names to faces was a lot more difficult.

I went to middle school the next year, and when I tried to make friends, I could never remember who was who. Remembering names and faces is a constant struggle to this day, but I do my best. Much later in life at a day program I attended, I remembered one participant's first name because she shared it with a famous actress. I asked her to introduce herself to me the next day using the actress' last name and I quickly remembered her first name!

In addition to impairing my memory, my brain injury made me very disorganized. In school, I found myself doing assignments twice because I would forget I had done them already. I prioritized assignments incorrectly—I would work on a big paper due in three months and forget about studying for tomorrow's quiz. I hated going to the library because I could never find anything. I was given copies of notes because I had difficulty taking notes from lectures. I also got a doctor's note to have extra time before the last period ended to go to my locker to organize what to bring home. Otherwise, I panicked and brought home the wrong things.

One of the biggest mistakes I made in school happened during seventh grade. I agreed to participate in an advanced placement program, which allowed me to go directly into high school the next year. I felt very awkward starting high school because my classmates were two years older than me (I had started first grade one year younger than the other students because I could read and do math already). I never fit in anywhere. If I would have continued that path, I would have graduated high school at sixteen. My mother realized I would struggle in college because I would be immature. When I started tenth grade, she convinced me to take an extra year of courses so I could mature. I started eleventh grade at fifteen years old and graduated high school when I was seventeen.

At age fourteen, something scary happened. I started to have very bad headaches and my vision developed a glare. I had difficulty focusing, developed poor depth perception and started seeing double. I had to cover one of my glasses' lenses with a cloth to block one of the images. This compensated for my double vision but couldn't correct the other problems. I went to the hospital and had a spinal tap to see how much pressure was inside of my head. They stuck a small needle into my spinal column through my lower back. This was an agonizing procedure. I remember at one point shouting, "sharp pain left foot!" This told the doctor to adjust the angle. The test registered four times the normal pressure on my brain. I was diagnosed with pseudo tumor cerebri. I had to have daily spinal taps to reduce the fluid around my brain and lower the pain. The problem was that more fluid would be produced again every day. To remedy this, a surgeon put a tube from my lower spinal column into my abdomen to drain cerebral fluid. It took the pain and double vision away immediately. I was grateful I no longer had to cover up one of my glasses' lenses with a cloth to block out one of the images.

The surgery was unable to remedy my focusing difficulty, glare and depth perception losses. My eye doctor diagnosed me with irreversible optic nerve damage. After I went back to school I realized how much my life was changed. Lessons were difficult because I could no longer see words on chalkboards or overheads. It also took me twice as long to read. The more I read, the quicker my vision deteriorated. Text was glary and I couldn't see contrasts at all. I had to lean in to see my computer. Prescription orange lenses made the glare worse. A few years later, I did get a driver's permit to see if I could safely drive. My first time behind the wheel, I knew it wasn't safe for me to drive because my vision was too blurry. It took a long time for me to accept this.

I am proud I overcame my struggles to graduate from high school, but I was extremely nervous about college. I was confused about what I *wanted* to do because I was so worried about what I *could* do. There were too many unanswered questions. What college would I attend? What would I major in? Because I could not drive, how would I get around? And finally, how would I be able to afford everything?

CHAPTER 4 –
My Successful Struggle
Through College

On May 12, 1996, I graduated with a Bachelor's degree in psychology from Utica College of Syracuse University. I remember more about my struggle getting through college than the courses themselves. As an example, one day a major paper was due. I panicked because I must never have seen it on the syllabus and had not done it. This is one example of how my brain injury causes me to miss important things in life.

I chose to further my education because I knew I wanted to be qualified to help people overcome challenges in their lives. I was very confused about what I would be able to do in life. I initially applied to the respiratory therapy program at Mohawk Valley Community College so I could make people with breathing problems feel better. Right before the semester was going to start, however, someone suggested my asthma would impede my ability to do the job. I ended up switching to Herkimer County Community College and read through their course book to see which majors interested me. I chose their physical therapy assistant program.

I passed my first semester's courses even though I wasn't comfortable doing any of the procedures. I was assigned to a local nursing home to get hands-on experience during my winter break. My supervisor there must have recognized my insecurity because I was never allowed to do much with residents. After one week, my college professor came by for an update. She talked with me briefly, met with my on-site supervisor privately then called me in to meet with them. I was nervous because I knew what they were about to say. My on-site supervisor told me I was never allowed to do very much because she was uncomfortable with my abilities. I was told I would have to discontinue the physical therapy program.

I set up a meeting with my academic advisor before college started. We discussed my disabilities at length and what I wanted to do with my life. I told her I wanted to help people with disabilities in some way. After reading the course book, we agreed I should switch to human services. From then on, courses were enjoyable and the next four semesters were easier. I finished all the credits for my two-year degree in December 1993.

Then I went on to Utica College of Syracuse University. Again, I thumbed through the course book for a major. I chose to major in child life psychology. I passed the courses my first semester and was excited about my upcoming hands-on experience at a local pediatric hospital.

Once again, I was never allowed to do very many activities with the children. As with my hands-on experience in physical therapy, my supervisor told me I was being restricted because she felt uncomfortable with my abilities. She also suggested I switch majors. I completely understood. This time, I selected general psychology. It was a struggle, but I passed all the courses and earned my degree. All my fellow graduates were excited about their futures. I was worried about mine.

CHAPTER 5 –
My Breakdown

I knew one semester before graduation that I would lose my step-father's health insurance coverage the day after I graduated college. To cover all my medical needs, I knew I would have to find a job with great health insurance. During winter break, I started looking through the Help Wanted ads day after day, sent out several resumes, made several phone calls and had some interviews. Nothing worked. I took each rejection hard. Depression entrenched itself into me deeper and deeper each day. During my last semester, I started to panic because I had no idea what my future held. All of this was very difficult because it was by far the most challenging semester I ever had.

The entire summer after graduation was fraught with one let-down after another in my search for a job. All I could do was comb the Help Wanted Ads day after day and hope for the best. Transportation was a huge issue because we lived far away from local businesses, there were no bus routes I could easily access and taxis cost way beyond what I could afford. I needed help.

In the fall, I got hooked up with a man who helped people with disabilities find appropriate jobs. I didn't seek his help at first because I thought my degree alone would work. After a few meetings, he set me up working as a child care aide in three area schools. I didn't know whether I could do it, but accepted it because I was desperate.

Running activities was very difficult because of my memory and organizational problems, and my asthma prevented me from playing along with the kids. I stuck with it because it was the only job I could find. About two months into it, however, my co-worker wrote a letter to our supervisor because she didn't feel comfortable working with me. I acknowledged her concerns and agreed to put in my resignation before they had a chance to fire me.

Several factors made my depression deepen more as each day passed. I needed to have some sort of income, so I had to go on welfare and food stamps. Every time I collected money, I felt ashamed because my value system taught me that people are supposed to earn their way, not just receive cash. I also hated having to rely on my mom and step-father for transportation. Every time I applied for a job, I would get a different excuse. I soon sought out counseling for my depression. This was particularly frustrating because there were no Medicaid-funded services available. This forced me to pay out-of-pocket (I had been on Medicaid since I graduated college).

One day, I got a letter from a federal program called Supplemental Security Income (SSI). It gives financial payments to individuals who can't work. I had applied for this benefit before I finished college because my mom was concerned about how I would support myself after I graduated. I walked into my bedroom and opened the letter. My case was denied again (they had turned me down once before). I cried for a few minutes, wiped away the tears, and showed it to my mom. She gave me some encouragement but it didn't help.

As evening rolled around, it was time to take my pills. After I got a drink, I walked back into my room. I picked up the pill bottle. It spoke to me. "Michael, I'm the answer to all of your problems."

"Hmm," I sighed. "I don't know."

"You'll just fall asleep and never have anything to worry about anymore."

I started crying. I dumped the bottle of pills into my hand and grabbed my drink. Mom must have known what I was doing because just then she walked into my room.

"You are coming with me," she cried.

"Where are we going?" I asked.

"I'm taking you to the Emergency Room. I'm not going to just sit back and watch you do something stupid."

She took me to the Emergency Room. I told them how badly I felt and what I had done. Immediately, a security guard came to my room to monitor me. After I talked with the psychiatrist on call, an ambulance brought me to a crisis residence. I shared my room with a man who was curled up on his bed, mumbling to himself. It didn't bother me because I thought I was finally going to get the help I desperately needed.

As nighttime approached, the Lord spoke to me. I started a conversation with a janitor working near my bed. I don't know why I felt so comfortable talking with him but I told him what had happened and how I was feeling. I will never forget the five words of encouragement he gave me.

"Sometimes you just gotta believe." I heard them over and over in my head as I drifted off to sleep. I slept better than I had in years. The next day, I knew things would all work out. I knew it was the Lord speaking through the janitor to let me know if I trust Him, I could get through anything. I was a completely new person because I knew my Lord had big plans for me. I couldn't wait to see how He would make them happen!

The next week, in a paper called *The Hamilton County News*, there was an ad for an income-subsidized apartment in Indian Lake, the small town where I grew up. It would be a safe place for me to learn what it would take to be independent. It didn't take long for my application to be processed and approved. My family helped me prepare and on Friday, May 30, 1997, I moved out on my own! Before going to sleep that first night in my new place, I thanked the Lord for everything He had done to make it happen.

CHAPTER 6 –
Living Independently
Is Hard

I never realized how many challenges I would have to overcome until I was living on my own. I couldn't remember where I put things, so I taped big, bold hand-made labels all over my apartment. This took a lot of time, but I loved not having to guess where things were. I replaced these labels with fancier, computer-generated ones a couple of years later.

I also had to come up with a way to organize my schedule. I wrote each day of the month on individual sheets of paper and stapled them together. As things came up, I applied sticky notes to the appropriate page. Each evening, I would remove the notes from the next day's page and write a chronological list of everything I needed to do, from getting up and taking morning pills right through taking medication at bedtime. I crossed off each day's items as they were finished, which gave me a way to remember what I had and had not done. This was especially important if something unexpected happened because I get very forgetful if I am distracted.

I remember very little of what people tell me. This makes using a telephone extremely difficult because as soon as I hang up, I can't remember anything about the conversation. I found a two-way recorder to put both sides of my conversations onto cassettes so I could transcribe them. It blew me away the first time I used it because I finally had a way to remember my conversations. I started making handwritten transcripts of every call I made or received. This took a *lot* of time, but made life a lot easier.

I also needed to find a way to remember what I talked about with people in person. I purchased a pocket recorder for this. I used it to make transcripts of all important meetings. I also used it throughout my day to give myself reminders. At the end of each day, I followed up on my recordings then deleted them. I would recommend these portable recorders to anyone who needs help remembering things.

I had to learn how to manage my medications properly. I knew which pills and inhalers to take and when they were due, but had to remember whether I had taken them. As soon as I got up,

I took my morning medications and put my evening pills into a small container I carried around all day. When pills were due, I took them. As I emptied my pockets at the end of the day, I threw the empty pill container in a chair with other items I carried around. Once in a great while, it rattled when I emptied my pockets, so I knew I had forgotten them earlier and took them late. It was a simple system, but worked well.

My independence is also limited because I cannot drive. As I discussed earlier, at one point I did get a learner's permit because all I had to do was pass a written test and a vision exam at the Department of Motor Vehicles. I was nervous, but gave driving a shot. It wasn't long before I realized it was not safe. I was so focused on staying between the lines on the road, I could easily have caused an accident.

I needed to devise some strategies to do grocery shopping. I made an aisle-by-aisle map listing every item I bought regularly at the grocery store. Before I went shopping, I inventoried my apartment and wrote down everything I needed and where things could be found. I had to do this strategy every time I shopped. Being able to shop independently was very rewarding.

I hope all of this gave you a glimpse into how challenging it was for me to move out on my own. I use the word "challenging" instead of "difficult" because the harder things became, the stronger my resolve to overcome them grew. I refused to let things keep me down for very long because if I did, it would mean I let them win. Nothing will ever beat me!

CHAPTER 7 –
My Victory with
The Government

I already talked about getting rejected for Supplemental Security Income, the government program that pays benefits to people who can't work. My mom and I filed an appeal, but another reviewer also rejected my claim. We appealed again, this time with legal help, but didn't hear anything. We abandoned it.

In April of 1999, however, I got a call from an administrative law judge. This person was responsible for reviewing disability claim appeals. I told him I was surprised to hear from him because I had assumed my case was closed. He asked me a few questions. A while later, I received a letter from SSI informing me I had finally won my case! Apparently, this judge found an old claim from April 1995, and because SSI back-pays its awards to the date of the original claim, the award was for forty-eight months and came to almost seventeen thousand dollars! I went from getting by on welfare and food stamps to having a fortune at my disposal!

I found out something disturbing at that point, however. For Medicaid to continue covering my health care expenses, I could not have more than $2000 in the bank. I would have to make a lot of purchases to get my resources below that figure. For the first time in my life, money was no object! I replaced all my furniture and household items. I bought an entirely new wardrobe. I hired an expensive computer consultant and purchased a high-end computer with all the accessories. I purchased a *lot* of take-out food. I ate out a lot! Somehow, I successfully spent down my resources in the time required, but would have preferred to save it for a rainy day.

I hope my story has encouraged any of you who may be battling through an SSI case to be as vigilant with it as I was.

CHAPTER 8 –
Nothing Is Wrong with
Wanting More

As much as I loved being independent, it was very difficult to compensate for all my difficulties and get everything done. One of my family members thought the agency for which she worked could help. The agency's name was Sunmount Developmental Disabilities Services Organization. I did everything necessary and became eligible for their support.

I was assigned to a Medicaid Service Coordinator who wrote a plan documenting my life history, giving specifics about how my disability limited my functioning and suggesting supports to help me. I was excited because I thought I would finally get the help I needed to make my life easier. I told him I was interested in volunteering with people with disabilities. In our discussion, I mentioned I played a keyboard. He set me up playing three times a week for people with disabilities who received Sunmount services in different settings.

I became frustrated because I never received the amount of help I needed in my home. I needed help with organizational skills, money management and running errands. Realizing his agency would not be able to help because no staff could be found, my service coordinator helped me switch to another agency, the Adirondack Arc.

I got a new Medicaid Service Coordinator through the Adirondack Arc and looked forward to getting direct care support. I thought I would have people helping me run errands, which really would have been handy during inclement weather. I also thought I would have ongoing help keeping my schedule organized. And I hoped someone would finally assist me with my checkbook. I did receive in-home services from a few people, but the agency had difficulty retaining people and there were long periods of time I had no staff. It wasn't long before I realized how limited my opportunities were in Indian Lake.

I quickly grew very lonely in Indian Lake. Because my apartment was one mile from the center of town, the only way for me to socialize would be to take two long walks. The weather always had to be factored in, and most of the social opportunities happened in the evenings. Walking that far in the dark was not possible because of my vision problems, so I spent all my evenings by myself.

I knew I would have to relocate. I set up a meeting with my Medicaid Service Coordinator to consider my options. He suggested moving to Saranac Lake, a slightly larger town almost two hours away. I was amazed when we first went there because my apartment building would be right in town, there were only a few streets to navigate and the town was quite compact. I could easily walk anywhere. My mom was hesitant to support me at first, but eventually realized it was in my best interest.

I was blown over by how many services I received in the new county. Four times per week, direct care staff helped me run errands and keep organized. An employment agency for individuals with disabilities started working with me and set me up in a custodial job where they gave me rides to and from work. It was part of a work program where people with disabilities were paid a percentage of minimum wage based on how fast they worked. These supports made me realize my move was a great idea, even though I didn't like being so far away from my family.

After I was there for almost one year, one of my co-workers left our crew to start bagging groceries in a large supermarket. Her success made me think I could do the same. I applied and was hired to work four six-hour shifts per week. It felt great to earn minimum wage for the first time!

I also needed a better way to worship the Lord because going to the Catholic church for one service each week just wasn't enough for my growing need. To fill my void, I became a Eucharistic minister there, handing out wafers and wine during services a couple times each month. This helped but still didn't fill the void. I considered other area churches and started attending a bible study at the local Methodist Church on Sunday mornings. A few weeks later, I also started attending the North Country Christian Center by catching a cab immediately after the Methodist Church bible study and arriving just before the one at the center started. This meant I had to switch going to Catholic mass on Saturdays because Sunday morning was busy!

One day, I was walking by the park close to my apartment and saw a crowd listening to a Christian music band. After listening for a while, a nice elderly gentleman approached me and told me they belonged to a church in a nearby town. He invited me to come with him to their Sunday evening service. I enjoyed it because it was a longer service and it had a nice church band. I started attending each Sunday evening, but continued to attend my other services. One evening, the pastor's son was preaching. I don't remember anything about his sermon but remember after he finished, I had an overpowering need to receive prayer. At the end of the service, parishioners could receive personalized prayer at the front of the church. I shivered as he spoke a word from the Lord to me. I accepted the Lord as my Savior that night. I have lived for Him ever since.

CHAPTER 9 –
I Don't Want to See
Jesus Yet!

Sunday, July 4, 2004 was a day I will never forget. I woke up with the worst headache of my life. It felt like an atom bomb had exploded inside of my head. I took my morning pills along with two Tylenol and cancelled my ride to church. I prayed to the Lord to take away my agony, and went back to bed. It was much worse when I woke up. I was in so much pain I could hardly stand up straight, but got dressed, called a cab and went to the E.R. I was there for a couple of hours and was sent home with a painkiller. I spent the entire day in bed. The next morning, the pain was much worse. I returned to the E.R., was given a stronger painkiller with a sleeping element and was sent home again. I took it and went right to bed. I prayed to the Lord to either take away my agony or take my life.

When I woke up the next morning, I couldn't stand the pain any longer. I very slowly got dressed, called a taxi and went to the E.R. for the third time. This time, they took a CAT scan of my head. A few moments later, I was approached by three medical professionals with my results. I had a ruptured cerebral aneurysm. In other words, a blood vessel had burst inside my head. They would have to fly me to Fletcher-Allen Health Care in Burlington, Vermont to have surgery to save my life.

"I need to let my mom know!" I cried.

"How far away does she live?" One of the doctors asked.

"She is at her camp in Raquette Lake right now. It's about an hour and a half away."

"If she leaves right away, she will get here just before you leave."

The doctors called her and told her what was happening. She asked to speak to me. As soon as I picked up the phone, I cried out, "I don't want to see Jesus yet!" She said she'd pack a change of clothes, her pills and her oxygen and try to meet me before I flew out. The doctors told her to hurry. Within two hours, I was rolled to the roof of the hospital where the Life Flight helicopter was running. Mom was right there waiting to see me. As my stretcher was rolled into the helicopter, I again cried to her "I don't want to see Jesus yet!" And with those words, we flew off.

During the procedure to tie off the ruptured blood vessel inside of my head, something very serious happened: I had a stroke. This prevented the surgeons from repairing my aneurysm that day. The surgery was redone successfully the next day and the crippling headache stopped. I was grateful to finally have relief.

I soon realized how severely the stroke had weakened my body. Because it occurred on the left side of my brain, the right side of my body was affected. I lost my ability to smile and exhibit facial expressions because my right cheek muscles stopped working. I could no longer raise my right arm higher than my shoulder, and I had extreme difficulty holding onto things like eating or writing utensils with my right hand because the joint in my thumb and one of the joints in my right pointer finger stiffened. I was told I could either learn to use my left hand for everything or force myself to regain strength and mobility in my right hand. I learned to carry items by grasping onto them with my right hand, flipping them over and carrying them from underneath. Physical therapy also helped me regain normal functioning. As the weeks went on, my fingers strengthened and my shoulder became more flexible. There was no way I was about to let that stroke keep me down!

Because my family and I were uncomfortable with me moving back into my apartment after I was discharged, I chose to live with them at their summer camp. I didn't lose any of my supports during the whole ordeal. I retained my service coordinator, staff supervisor and my approved staffing hours. I kept my apartment during the summer even though I was away. Because my family had to move out of camp after Labor Day, my support team met a few times to discuss my future. My support team and I didn't feel comfortable with me living by myself right away, so I chose to build up to that by temporarily living in a two-bedroom house in Saranac Lake owned and staffed by the Adirondack Arc. I needed more than the eight hours of staffing I received at home and this was the only way the agency could provide it to me without going through the long process to formally approve increased hours.

I started out with staff twenty-four hours a day. This gave my team, my family and me the opportunity to see what kinds of supports I would need to live independently. They supervised my cooking and household duties and monitored how well I organized on my computer to make sure I was gaining my independence back. I started to freak out because I was not used to having so much staff. I missed the privacy. I walked back to my old apartment one day, opened my door, and a calm came over me. It was as if God told me, "It won't be long before you're home."

CHAPTER 10 –
A Short Road to Recovery

I worked hard to regain my independent living skills during those weeks. I knew once I was back on my own again, I would only have limited staffing. I started organizing my schedule on Microsoft Outlook. I started transcribing all my calls again. I forced the two fingers that would not bend to hit their proper keys, even though it would have been easier using other fingers. I took long walks to rebuild my leg strength. I proved to everyone, including myself, that I could do my own cooking, cleaning and laundry. It would have been very easy for me to allow my staff to fill some of these roles, but I chose to be more independent.

I also started physical therapy to bring back the mobility of my right shoulder and the strength and flexibility of my right hand. Forcing my stiff shoulder to stretch normally was very uncomfortable at first but I knew it had to happen. I was also given a rubber ball to squeeze to strengthen my right hand. This gradually brought back my grasp strength. But the weirdest thing was when a "zap gun" was used to apply mild electrical stimulation to my right cheek muscles to bring back my smile.

I had to show that I could independently manage my medications properly. My staff watched each morning as I took them and put my evening pills into a small bottle kept in my pocket to take in the evening. It wasn't long before I was trusted to manage my own medications again. I needed to do this to be able to move back on my own.

A couple weeks after moving into the Adirondack Arc house, my team and I realized I no longer needed overnight staffing. They started showing up at 8:00 a.m. and leaving at 8:00 p.m. This was a huge step because I proved to everyone I didn't need a lot of staff anymore and was on the way toward independence.

About three weeks after moving there, I returned to work at the supermarket. As thrilled as I was to be back, doing the job was a lot harder than it was before my stroke. I had to pick up items, quickly flip my hand over so I was carrying them from underneath, then put them into bags. My right shoulder and hand were weak, and my fingers did not bend well enough to do the job normally at first. As time went on, they regained normal flexibility and I got back my shoulder and hand strength. That job was excellent physical therapy!

Everyone soon realized I needed to have the chance to move back into my apartment. A couple of team meetings were set up with my family and support staff. Step-by-step, everything fell into place and on October 28, 2004, I moved back into my apartment. I will never forget those seven weeks of my life.

CHAPTER 11 --
Back on My Own Again

I never realized how much I enjoyed everything in my apartment until I had four months without it. From using my own towels, to eating on my own plates, to relaxing in my own chair, things were finally back to normal. I had my independence back. I could take a walk and no one asked where I was going and what time I'd return. I ran most of my errands and did everything necessary to be on my own. I had up to eight hours of staff support per week to help me stay organized and run big errands. This was much better than having staff all day long.

However, all those freedoms came with responsibilities. Unlike in the Adirondack Arc house where I had staff to bring me to appointments and do errands, I had to coordinate buses, taxis and other rides. I had to organize my own medications again. Whenever difficulties arose, I was now the one who had to deal with them. None of this was easy, but I was determined to make it work.

Just like when I was in Indian Lake, I was lonely being by myself most of the time in Saranac Lake. I usually had no one to talk to. I wished I had a girlfriend. To increase social contact, I took long walks around town. I also spent a large amount of time each week at church. I tried to keep busy at home because my loneliness was much worse when I had down time.

I enjoyed my job at the supermarket because it got me out of the apartment and had the strict routine I needed to overcome my memory problems, but I wished I had a job geared more toward my passion: helping folks with disabilities. In 2006, I joined the Franklin County Community Services Board and served on one of its subcommittees. They met in Malone, which meant I rode one hour each way with the Franklin County Community Services Director. As the months went on, she got to know me better and started asking questions about where I thought my life was going. I told her I'd always wanted a job helping people with disabilities and how my dream job would involve helping them learn how to speak up for themselves better. We contacted a woman who enrolled me in an eighteen-month state internship program through which I could start working. All the necessary steps were taken and in February 2007, I began working as the self-advocacy coordinator through Franklin County Community Services. I was very excited because it was my first professional job.

Job coaching services were provided for me while I was orienting myself because my brain injury makes organizing very difficult. I began leading a weekly group at a local day treatment center for persons with developmental disabilities. I also began a monthly group in Saranac Lake, and eventually started using a county bus to travel an hour to Malone to lead another group. Because I was never able to draw very many people to my meetings, my frustration increased as each month passed. I accepted my boss' solution to move my office into her building so she could keep a closer eye on things, but it did not help. By then, I had lost confidence in my ability to do the job. Group members caught on to this and lost interest in the groups. This increased my frustration even more. I started down-spiraling.

I don't recall exactly what the final straw was, but I remember at one point sending my boss an email telling her I had made the decision to resign. She came to my office and told me how to make it official. I couldn't help worrying about what my future held.

I contacted my employment service and after several meetings, I started working in a ritzy hotel on a laundry crew. It excited me because I knew I would be doing the same things again and again, which was perfect because I perform routine tasks very well. It was extremely fast-paced work because there were always mounds of linens and towels to clean. I was pressured to work very quickly. We had to visually scan all clean items before folding them to make sure they had no leftover stains. Because my poor eyesight made this very difficult, I often would fold dirty items as if they were clean. At one point, a spotted pillowcase was intentionally put in my pile to see if I would catch it but I didn't. There was no way to fix this problem, so I put in my resignation.

After quitting, I realized I had more work obstacles than I had considered. I took this very hard. I decided to stop looking for work and get therapy to address the anxiety and stress these disappointments had created.

This was an interesting period in my life because I had a lot of ups and downs. I went from being excited about the self-advocacy job to getting let down by it. Then I was excited about the routine job in the laundry but then my vision disability let me down. My mood became very unstable during this time. Little did I realize it would shortly have an incredible lift!

CHAPTER 12 –
My Miracle from The Lord

After mom went to see the Lord, I am confident the first thing she did was thank Him for relieving her of her pain. I am confident that she also asked him for a favor. "My son, Michael, is very lonely down there. Can you please set him up with a nice woman?" I am certain that the Lord told her, "Suzanne, you don't need to say it. I already know it." With those words, the path toward my miracle had begun.

Here is the story of how I met my wife Cheryl. We met in late September

2008 and got married on Saturday, October 3, 2009. Here is our story.

I never showed interest in dating during high school or college because I was completely focused on passing courses. After I moved out on my own, I grew very lonely because I was spending so much time by myself. I had no opportunities to develop a real friend. Many days, the only conversations I had were on the phone. I enjoyed running errands because they gave me more human contact. If I didn't have an errand to run, I went on long walks every day anyway because they got me out of the apartment.

During this time, I first noticed an interest in female companionship. Unlike most people who have this happen in their teens, I was in my mid 20's. One day, I bumped into a woman I knew from elementary school and we had fun sharing memories. She gave me her phone number, so I was hoping it would lead to something. I called her a couple of times over the next few days but she never returned my messages. I continued to be lonely for female companionship for several years.

My loneliness was a little better after I moved to Saranac Lake because there was more for me to do. Still, evenings were always hard because I wished I had a woman in my life. I started going out to local bars on weekends hoping for the best. I felt very out of place and hardly spoke with anyone, but at least I was around people. The bar scene never worked. Once, I took out a woman from church, but it never led to anything. God knew how lonely I was. He had better plans!

Through my self-advocacy job, I had been participating in a monthly video conference to share ideas with other self-advocacy groups. It was hard for me to report progress my groups were making because they were struggling. This made me feel insecure. I shared this feeling with others in the video conference. One day, I received a call from the regional field assistant of the Self-Advocacy Association of New York State to see if she could help. Her name was Cheryl. I opened up with her about all the difficulties I was experiencing.

She called me again in a couple of days and we talked for a while. We soon started having calls most evenings after work and most mornings. Our phone calls quickly grew in length. I had to stop transcribing her calls because I did not have enough time to keep up with them. One time my smoke alarm went off because I forgot something in the oven while talking with her! Another one of our calls was almost seven hours long—this made my phone bill over $200.00! We had to meet each other in person!

Neither of us had a vehicle and we lived one hundred miles apart, so we knew we'd have to use the bus to see each other. I had only used it once before. How would I make sure I didn't get off at the wrong stop? How would I remember to get my luggage off the bus? When I got off, how would I know who Cheryl was? After all, I didn't know what she looked like! As the bus pulled into the station in Glens Falls, my heart was racing.

Cheryl had thought ahead. She had a picture of me from one of my past self-advocacy newsletters, so she recognized me as I walked off the bus. When we got to her apartment, I was greeted by Cheryl's best friend—an eleven-year old Shiba-Inu Husky named Shelly. She barked at me at first but quickly quieted down. Cheryl and I stayed up very late getting to know each other. That evening, she gave me something I really needed at 34 years old: my first kiss!

The next morning, we went to the Self-Advocacy State Conference. I remember little about the event, but will never forget how great it felt spending time with her. By this point, we realized our relationship would only become stronger as time went on. After the three-day conference ended, we came back to her place. The next day, I presented to her self-advocacy group. The following day, we took the bus back to Saranac Lake.

Over the next month and a half, Cheryl came up to stay with me a few times. Cheryl wanted to go to the Baptist Church one Sunday, so we started walking. It was a mile and a half away and I had never been there before. It started snowing right after we left, and intensified the whole trip. When we arrived, the only person there was a man doing some cleaning. He welcomed us and told us his name was Kevin. He told us about Harold Clark, his dad, the pastor of the church. We did not meet his dad because he was away that day. As everyone started showing up, we were made to feel right at home. Kevin even gave us a ride home.

Throughout this period, we continued our long phone calls. It became clear that I loved her. During one call, we talked about how I planned to propose to her one day. We'd go to a fancy restaurant where I'd get down on one knee and pop the question. This never happened. I didn't know how to tell her I loved her because I didn't know whether she loved me back. At one point, I said, "I don't need to say it.

I think you already know it." She took it as a proposal!

We soon realized we could no longer be apart, so we started making plans for her to move in with me. I went down to Hudson Falls over Thanksgiving. Before we ate, each of us thanked God we would never be lonely again.

Cheryl moved in with me on Saturday, December 13th. Pastor Harold made it very clear that it was the appearance of evil for us to live together unmarried. Over the next three months, he told us our love would grow much deeper if we started living the Lord's way. We loved being with each other all the time but realized we shouldn't have moved in together before we were married. Cheryl moved into an apartment down the hall from mine on the other side of the elevators. When her dog, Shelly got off the elevator, she never could figure out which way to turn!

On Saturday, October 3, 2009, we got married. Many people are nervous on their wedding day, but I wasn't. I was excited about my new life with Cheryl. I knew Mom was smiling down on us from Heaven. The service and reception were held in different rooms in our church. We chose not to see each other until the wedding started.

The service started and the pianist started playing. Pastor asked me for the marriage certificate and rings. I realized something bad had happened – I HAD FORGOT THEM! My jaw dropped, I put my hands over my face and walked out of the church with my brother to go back to my apartment for them. We returned twenty minutes later and discovered our Pastor had led a praise music sing-a-long while we were gone. Cheryl joked with me afterwards: "It wouldn't have been a 'Michael Northrop wedding' unless something was forgotten!" We chose to videotape our service because it would bring back memories for us throughout our marriage, and every time I see that clip, I still get a little embarrassed!

Cheryl was more beautiful than I had ever seen her. She was wearing a white skirt suit and I was wearing a black three-piece suit. I wasn't used to seeing her face with so much make-up on! When we met, I told her she was beautiful without anything on her face. Her mom and sister had taken her to a beauty parlor before the ceremony.

Because Cheryl and I are very frugal, we tried to keep the costs of our wedding down. Our pastor did not charge us for his services and let us use the church for free because we each did a lot of volunteer work at church. We did not have to provide any of the food because it was a pot luck dinner. One of the pastor's daughters prepared our cake at a very reasonable cost. We didn't have to pay for any entertainment because our pastor agreed to perform during our service. It was a beautiful song called *The Broken Rose*, by Squire Parsons.

It has now been several years since our wedding and our love grows deeper each day. Before we go to sleep at night, we always tell each other "I love you". We help each other by doing just enough for each other but not too much. If I ask her a question, for example, instead of giving me the answer, she will give me clues which help me figure out the answer myself. But most importantly, we respect everything about each other, from limitations due to our disabilities, to how we manage money, to personal issues. We are truly a perfect pair.

We have adapted hand signs to communicate our feelings toward each other. In American Sign Language, you can communicate "I Love You" by holding your middle and ring finger down while extending your pointer finger and pinky and sticking out your thumb, (see image). I thought of a unique way to compliment it. I created my own sign. You stick out your ring and middle fingers and keep the other three down. I call it the "I Tolerate You" sign. One of us will do the I Love You sign, then the other will do the I Tolerate You sign and we will put our hands together. They fit together perfectly! It's one of the ways we communicate our love to each other. I proudly tell people the Lord is the best thing that ever happened to me but that Cheryl is a close second!

"I LOVE YOU"

"I TOLERATE YOU"

"LOVE TOLERANCE HANDSHAKE"

CHAPTER 13 –
Two Recent Opportunities in My Life

When I moved away from home, I knew I needed help organizing my life, managing finances and compensating for my memory disability. I sought out support services from New York State. I received Medicaid Service Coordination (MSC) to manage them. I was entitled to in-home supports to give me assistance running errands, managing money and staying organized, but no one was available to provide those supports. Switching to the Adirondack Arc one year later wasn't much better, so I realized I would have to move to get more support. I asked my MSC to help me find somewhere else to live where more opportunities would be available. He said a larger town would be better for me. He brought me to his home town, Saranac Lake, about an hour and a half away. I chose to move there, and started getting direct care help in my home right away. This was one of the best decisions I have ever made. I was pleased with my services for the next eleven years.

In 2012, I switched my services from the Adirondack Arc to the Department of Health Traumatic Brain Injury Waiver, which is for adults with head injuries. I received direct care supports and service coordination in both systems but qualified for specialized supports in the TBI waiver. One is called Independent Living Skills

Training (ILST) and is designed to train people with traumatic brain injuries to become more independent. I chose to use this support to help me learn how to edit the original version of this book, minimizing the effect my brain injury had on my writing. My ILST helps me use my laptop to organize my budget, email and calendar. I also receive two hours per week of Community Integration Counseling, which is designed to help me learn how to handle issues related to my brain injury and integrate back into my community. For two years, I participated in the North Country Regional Traumatic Brain Injury Center Structured Day Program in Plattsburgh, New York. I benefitted from a weekly cognitive therapy group, went bowling, participated in a writing group and enjoyed trips each week.

Here is the other big opportunity from which I have benefitted. After my failures in my self-advocacy job and my laundry job, I stopped looking for work. Then in early 2015, I reactivated my case with Career Visions Employment Service, an agency that helps people with disabilities find jobs appropriate for them. It always used to bother me when people would ask me what I do for a living and I had nothing to tell them.

In the process of looking for work, I learned a very valuable lesson. In my first three or four interviews, I was far too narrow-minded about my abilities, focusing too intently on the limitations involved with my brain injury. The first time a job duty sounded too much for me, I would rashly say "I can't do it," and the interview would end right there. It took a lot of effort from my team of supports (my wife, the job people, one of my in-home workers and my counselor) to convince me to be more open-minded toward possibilities. This open-mindedness allowed me to be hired at my current job.

I currently work for the Olympic Regional Development Authority (ORDA) in Lake Placid, New York. I was hired in September 2015 as one of the custodial crew. The building is enormous, so I was concerned about how I would find my way around. My job coach solved this problem by creating a set of cards with turn-by-turn directions I could flip through. I used them religiously at first, but it wasn't long before I knew my way around without them.

ORDA is the best job I have ever had. Everyone respects each other, from the executive director right down to all of us custodians. There is nice comradery between all of us custodians. When I first started, they helped me find my way around because they could see I was disoriented. Now I am rarely told what to do because they trust I will always make constructive use of my time. This trust is priceless. One time, someone bought me lunch when I forgot to bring my own. It is a good job for me.

PART TWO –

My Lessons In Life

CHAPTER 14 –
I Try Not to Let
Opportunities Pass Me By

Now I will tell you about several meaningful opportunities I have taken advantage of in my life and what each has meant. I hope they motivate you to think more openly about options you have as well.

I was very worried about what my future held after high school. I thought higher education would help me secure my future, so I chose to attend a local community college. I used the academic support center to help me in courses where I was having difficulty. After I graduated, I transferred to a four-year college because I knew I couldn't get a good enough job with a two-year degree. I graduated with my Bachelor's degree on May 12, 1996.

After moving on my own in 1997, I took advantage of different volunteer opportunities. While I was living in Indian Lake, I played my keyboard for people with disabilities three times each week in different settings. I loved sharing my musical gift with others. Then in Saranac Lake, I played for local agencies and called bingo at the Saranac Lake Adult Center. This volunteer work made me feel good.

In 2014, I participated on a panel made up of people with disabilities where we presented our stories to professionals at a local hospital. It was entitled "Focus on Our Similarities, Not Our Differences," and discussed how important it was not to treat us differently than other people. We talked about how others have reacted to us because of our disabilities. We were warmly received and presented again in 2015.

I accepted offers to participate on several boards of directors and committees designed to improve the lives of people with disabilities. Shortly after I began to receive their services, I joined the Board of Directors of the Adirondack Arc. I became a member of a subcommittee of the Hamilton County Services Board. In 2002, I joined the human rights committee of the Adirondack Arc and was also elected to the board of directors of the Self-Advocacy Association of New York State. I was elected to the Franklin County Community Services Board in 2007 and then appointed to one of its subcommittees a few months later. A few years later, I became a board member of the Tri-Lakes Center for Independent Living and functioned as its president for a while. These opportunities are very rewarding because they allow me to advocate on behalf of people receiving services.

I have always sought assistance to make life as easy as possible. Since moving to Saranac Lake in 2001, I have taken advantage of many different supports and services to help me. My Medicaid Service Coordinator oversees all my care. In-home services help me stay organized, run errands, and maintain my budget. Community Integration Counseling helps control my stresses and Independent Living Skills Training teaches me valuable skills to increase my independence.

I took advantage of several opportunities to get jobs during my life.

Shortly after moving away from home, I eagerly accepted an offer to clean my apartment complex. It was the first job I ever had. As it turned out, I enjoyed doing custodial work. In 2002, I enrolled in a sheltered workshop program where people with disabilities were given supervised jobs doing things like gardening, maintenance and cleaning. I was assigned to the evening custodial crew. I showed everyone I can succeed at a more involved job if given the right supports. The five years bagging groceries at a super market was my first opportunity to prove I could succeed in a regular job. My self-advocacy job was an opportunity to help people with disabilities learn how to speak up for themselves. And ORDA is an opportunity for me to feel highly respected as part of a team where everyone helps each other.

My romance with Cheryl is the best example of how I took advantage of a few opportunities. I was having some difficulties at work and she offered me some assistance. Every evening on the phone, she was an excellent sounding board for me to vent problems I had at work. I very quickly felt comfortable sharing personal stories with her and she reciprocated her personal stories back to me just as freely. Soon, we started sharing our faith with each other and began praying together as part of each phone call. As our love for each other intensified, so did our love for the Lord.

These examples have one thing in common. I didn't sit back and let things happen—I took things into my own hands. It is scary for anyone to do this, but it is especially terrifying for people with disabilities because it is a lot easier to sit back and let people do things for us. There is a huge risk if you make changes in your life, but I think it's worth taking the chance. So, whatever your options may be, please take them into serious consideration.

CHAPTER 15 – My Failures Are Only Successes in Disguise

Someone once told me failures teach more than successes. I never thought it made sense, but now I understand. This chapter discusses several times in my life where I have struggled through difficult things and achieved successes.

I never let my disability deter my education. At age ten, instead of letting my new brain injury devastate my life, I used it as a motivation. I came up with ways to move past it and graduate elementary school. One of my most useful tools in junior high was note cards. I would put a question on one side and the answer on the other and just keep flipping through them often. I used note cards more frequently in high school. Although physical therapy and child life psychology never worked out for me, I am proud I graduated with my Bachelor's Degree in psychology.

Soon after I moved out on my own, I figured out many ways to compensate for my disabilities. Shopping was extremely difficult because I could never remember where things were found and couldn't quickly scan for them due to poor vision. I made an aisle-by-aisle map of where to find every item I purchased regularly. I also kept sticky-notes by my refrigerator so I could mark down items I needed to buy. I created a list I brought to the store of all items I needed and where to find them. If I did not go to all this effort, I had no way to remember items I needed or where they were found. It was also very difficult organizing my time and remembering what was going on from day to day. I started writing "To Accomplish Today" lists for things I needed to do and would cross items off as they were done. I made a lot of mistakes at first, but it organized my time because it helped me remember what I had and had not done yet.

My self-advocacy positon is my best example of how a failure became a blessing in disguise. Although the job only lasted five years and was loaded with disappointments, I met my amazing wife through it. God also used it to make me much more grounded in my evaluation of my abilities. I realize now the self-advocacy job was *way* out of my league.

This book itself is an excellent example of a failure in my life becoming a blessing in disguise. My original version was called *Escape from A Padded Cell*. When I sent it to my publisher, I never realized I had copied the text from chapter four and pasted it underneath the title for chapter six. I took most of the text from my original book and revised it in this book. Revising the original book also allowed me to include the things which had happened over the past decade.

I have overcome my problem remembering what people tell me in person and over the phone. I purchased a two-way recorder for my phone calls. I transcribe important calls onto a file on my computer so my wife and my staff can help me follow up on them. With my digital pocket recorder, I leave myself reminders of things I need to do. This compensates very well for my inability to remember things on the go, but I am still working on strategies to perfect my follow through from my reminders.

So as much as my successes may have stood out in my memories of life, the times I grew the most were from my failures.

CHAPTER 16 –
My Disability Makes Me
Who I Am

I would not want to know what life would be like without my disability. Many people are shocked when they hear this. My brain injury has made me who I am. I could feel sorry for myself, but I don't. On several occasions in my life, people have told me they are sorry for me because of everything I have gone through but I have always told them God used it all to make me who I am today. I always try to search for better ways to overcome my disabilities and grow stronger from them.

I have empathy for people with disabilities because of all I have experienced in my life. Many people feel sympathy, but it can't be empathy unless they have a disability too. For example, I know two people with Alzheimer's disease, which affects their memory severely. People feel sympathy for them because they are very forgetful, but I feel empathy for them because I have memory issues too.

I have always wanted to help improve the lives of people with disabilities. I loved the smiles I used to get from the consumers when I volunteered at the day habilitation centers in Hamilton County. I have enjoyed participating on the Adirondack Arc Board of Directors, its Human Rights Committee, and the Tri-

Lakes Center for Independent Living Board of Directors because they have allowed me to represent the people they serve.

My brain injury influenced my choice of a college major. In order to help improve the lives of people with disabilities, I majored in human services and psychology. I loved learning why people behave the way they do and how to influence their decisions. Psychology taught me a lot about dealing with my own stresses and how to help other people cope with theirs. I always wanted to learn more about how my disability affected my thinking; human services and psychology gave me the opportunities to do that. Although my injury prevented me from pursuing a professional career in my field, I have no regrets about going to college.

I have a strong desire to help people with and without disabilities see each other more equally. I have pursued this with my writings. The desire to move past my struggles and help others move past theirs has energized my passion for writing for a long time. During my self-advocacy job, I wrote a newsletter called *Speakin' Out* to give my readers a way to be heard. I have also written several articles called *Bridging the Gap*, highlighting ways people with and without disabilities can see each other more equally. I have put a lot of time and energy into this book and hope it helps people with and without disabilities—I would never have written it if I did not have a disability myself. I am proud my writing has been influenced so powerfully by the challenges I have overcome.

So please do whatever it takes to develop a positive perspective about your disability or people you know.

CHAPTER 17 –
My New Life with
Jesus Christ

My faith in the Lord Jesus Christ means everything to me. He has been with me my whole life, even when I didn't realize He was. After I considered suicide, He used the janitor in that crisis residence to tell me, "Sometimes, you just gotta believe." My relationship with the Lord has blossomed over the last two decades. He gave me my victory with the Supplemental Security Income program, helped me find another nice place to live, saved my life during the cerebral aneurysm, introduced me to Cheryl, qualified me for great supports and gave me a good job. I can't wait to see what He will do next!

The last time I read through *The Holy Bible*, I recorded onto a computer document hundreds of scriptures that were important to me. It ended up a little over two hundred pages long! I talk out loud with the Lord throughout each day and thank Him for every single thing He does. If the Lord and I had been this close in February 1997, I never would have considered suicide.

God allowed everything in my life to happen for a reason. The chapter discussing my brain injury was entitled "My Biggest Gift from God" because I know He allowed it to happen so I would learn how to empathize with others who have disabilities. Although it only lasted five years, I know the

Lord put me in my self-advocacy position so He could introduce me to Cheryl. He has given me a passion to use my writing to help others–I want my readers to learn from my experiences so they will not repeat my mistakes. And the Lord gave me the ability to play the piano by ear to entertain people. These gifts from the Lord are very important to me.

There have been two areas where the Lord has allowed me to grow from failed experiences. Although it seemed like an incredible opportunity at first, the failure of my self-advocacy position taught me I need a job with more concrete tasks, like the cleaning position I have now. And He used my wife and friends to convince me to step down as co-leader of our self-advocacy group because He knew I would benefit more from only being a member.

In hard times, we all need something to lean on. Asking the Lord for help takes a huge burden off my shoulders. I enjoy walking by myself because I talk out loud to my Lord wherever I go. I always give him thanks for everything He has done for me and pray for things I need. I also thank Him for things He has done for my wife and many other people and pray for His blessings over all of us. Every once in a while, He gives me an enjoyable shiver down my spine, undeniable proof He is there.

I hope I have not offended you by discussing my relationship with the Lord as explicitly as I have. I would never want to know where my life would have gone if I did not accept Him into my life twenty years ago.

CHAPTER 18 –
The Stuff I've Learned

I have learned several important lessons throughout my life. Because I had such severe health problems as a child, I had to learn to grow up quickly. Telling my mother exactly how I felt helped her figure out whether I needed a doctor's appointment or an emergency room trip. Then at age ten after I had the seizure, I learned how to compensate for my memory loss by saying things again and again, and coming up with funny words to help me memorize lists. In high school, for example, I learned the nine steps of cardiopulmonary resuscitation (CPR) by using "con-hope-pos-ope-che-bre-clear-look-call." When my vision was damaged at age fourteen, I had to develop adaptive skills. I had to learn to toe-touch when descending stairs because I could no longer see where each one ended. I also had to learn how to walk more cautiously to prevent tripping on uneven surfaces. I learned that accepting help in high school and college would make things easier. And by admitting it was difficult living on my own, I have benefitted from several services since 1999.

The most powerful lesson I ever learned happened in February 1997. I let the Lord take control of my life after I considered committing suicide. I learned to trust that He will guide the decisions I make in life. I realized none of them would be easy, but I knew He would be there for me the whole way.

Even to this day when problems creep up, my wife reminds me to simply look to Him. Then things always work out well.

Living in Indian Lake taught me some important lessons. I realized I needed to map out the grocery store so I could find things more easily. I never realized how badly I needed social opportunities until I was living in a place where there were so few. And because it was such a struggle to find enough support services, I realized I would have to relocate to meet my needs. These last two examples were the biggest reasons I chose to move to Saranac Lake.

I have learned some important lessons since I married Cheryl. I never shared my apartment with anyone before her, so I had to make a lot of adjustments. It took a while getting used to feeling someone sleeping next to me, particularly because she enjoys using a fan all night long. I started adjusting my schedule so we could share time alone together, switched which side of the bed I used so she could use her fan at night and adjusted my sleeping schedule to hers by going to sleep two hours earlier. I had to adjust my schedule around times the dog needed to go outside, get exercise, get food and water, and be taken care of, especially in her later years when she needed it most. And, most importantly, I learned the hard way never to compare Cheryl's cooking with mom's or grandma's!

Each of my jobs has taught me something about myself. My bagging job taught me I work very well with extreme routine. I thought my self-advocacy job would challenge my abilities more, but it showed me I am not able to handle a complex job. It grounded me a lot and forced me to take a realistic look at what I could do. I learned from my laundry job how my vision problems were more serious than I had expected. It took only two days in a motel cleaning position for me to realize I am not able to work in a very fast-paced environment. Since August 2015, I have had a job which never would have happened if I had remained inflexible and negative. Previously, I turned down several other jobs by creating roadblocks when I overemphasized obstacles instead of thinking positively. I was hired in September 2015 as a janitor for the Olympic Regional Development Authority in Lake Placid. I still work there and am proud I did not let my fears about orienting myself in such an enormous building keep me from success.

After switching to the TBI waiver, I found out I could attend a day program designed for individuals with traumatic brain injury. I was hesitant at first because of my experience with day programs; participants in those programs were never able to do very much because of their limitations. I traveled to the TBI Center Day Program in Plattsburgh to check it out. Programs were designed to improve social interaction and offer community access. There was a weekly cognitive therapy group to improve mental abilities. Wednesday afternoon was always fun because we went bowling, and Thursdays we went on fun field trips. After going to the center for three years, I now have a completely different view of what day treatment is like.

I have grown from all these experiences and hope you can open your mind to expand opportunities for yourself as well.

CHAPTER 19 –
A Work in Progress

I consider my life now a work in progress because there will always be areas to improve. Since we got married, Cheryl and I have promised to strengthen our love more each day. We completed couple's therapy to work on issues we were experiencing. We regularly cuddle in each other's arms. I am working on listening to her more. If I don't, she says "put a quarter in the jar." (The hospital where she volunteers gave her a coin jar to collect money for Relay for Life to support cancer research). These are just a couple ways we work on improving our marriage.

I have recently become aware of one area where I need to improve. I tend to view growth possibilities with a closed mind. This makes me miss out on potential opportunities which may have been available if I viewed my abilities more open-mindedly. About job possibilities, I tend to overestimate the impact my brain injury will have and underestimate how effectively I can compensate for it. In one interview, I rejected a janitorial job at a local adult center simply because I was told I needed to be flexible about what I did day to day. I also turned down two other jobs because I was not thinking about my abilities with an open mind.

My brain injury affects more than my memory and orientation. It makes me have a short fuse when I feel overwhelmed. My wife, my counselor and I have been working on strategies to alleviate tension in the moment. We have used deep breathing techniques, where my wife or others recognize I am very stressed and tell me to take a couple of slow, deep breaths. In the moments, it takes me to do this, not only am I getting more oxygen to my brain, time is passing and allowing me to forget about the stressor. Unfortunately, I admit I often ignore her suggestions and allow momentary stresses to build. I am working on this problem with her and my counselor, but I admit I still need to make a lot of improvement here. It is difficult for me to remember to use them when situations become tense because they have not yet become habitual. I need to improve how effectively I use these techniques.

Re-writing this book has been a great opportunity to improve the quality of my writing. Because my brain injury distorts how I organize my thoughts and words, I accepted many editorial suggestions from an author friend. At first, I was resistant to her but soon realized she only had my best interest in mind. I learned how to use bulleted lists to organize my thoughts and sentences. I even got to the point where I could generate them completely on my own. But most importantly, I benefitted from re-reading each word of this book, re-organizing my thoughts, simplifying my language and making everything as concise as possible.

I have also matured in the way I entertain people when I play music. At the Saranac Lake Adult Center where I volunteered regularly, I felt my playing was not being appreciated because I never got feedback from anyone during my performances. Several people suggested I develop a way to initiate interactions with my audience during the performances. I was very resistant but eventually agreed to give it a chance. The enjoyment of playing returned immediately by interacting with people more.

In June 2016, I relinquished my position as a leader of our self-advocacy group because I realized I still had to develop the skills needed for leadership. In retrospect, I realize this is one of the biggest reasons I failed in my job as self-advocacy coordinator. It is so much more fun participating in meetings instead of being expected to help lead them. Recognizing my limits and accepting them truly was a growth step for me.

Promoting this book is another example of a work in progress. There are a lot of things I must learn to do this effectively. Costs in all areas must be minimized. I hope to deliver presentations within the community, especially at the annual Brain Injury Association of New York State conference and the New York State Self-Advocacy Association conference. I need to learn Microsoft PowerPoint to do this and will use bullet lists to organize my thoughts.

At one point, I met with two Adirondack Arc executives to improve my performance on my board and committee. I felt there were areas where I was not fulfilling my role well enough. They reassured me I was doing fine. I am also on the board for an agency promoting independent living for folks with disabilities. This afforded me an unexpected growth opportunity. I perceived tension in the agency because we had to replace our executive director. I felt uncomfortable being on the board and considered resigning. After I had long talks with my wife and friends, I chose to stay on that board. I reviewed several résumés, came up with interview questions to ask and helped in hiring our new director. Our board had to do this process over again not much later to hire yet another director. With all of this, I again considered quitting but have again chosen to stay on and grow as a board member.

My life is like our planet. It is constantly evolving. I keep trying to come up with new ways to adapt. Just like our Grand Canyon is constantly deepening, I consider my life a work in progress. Guided by my Lord Jesus Christ, I can't wait to see what will happen next!

GOD'S LATEST GIFT

Three days after Christmas 2015, Cheryl and I took our dog Shelly to the vet for the last time. She lived to be eighteen years and three and a half months old. We gave ourselves one month to heal then decided to adopt another dog. We chose to adopt another rescue dog from the local animal shelter. This is his picture. His name is Melo and he is a two-year old corgi-dachshund mix. It was very difficult getting used to his energy because Shelly lost hers as she got older. Every day after work, I have a "lap buddy" as soon as

I sit down. And my wife and I have to throw two dog treats onto the floor to get him off my side of the bed! I loved Shelly for the seven years I shared with her and Cheryl and will love Melo for many years to come, too.

THE END

Made in the USA
Lexington, KY
17 August 2018